My Invention or My Idea

I wisdom dwell with prudence, and find out knowledge of witty inventions. PROVERBS 8:12 (KJV)

By Mareen Oliver

I Mareen Bland Peoples grew up on the west side of Chicago(K-Town) by the time I was 7 or 8 years old my parents had separated. At this time, I lived in a basement apartment with my mother and 3 siblings. The roaches and rats thought they lived there as well. I am the oldest of the four children my mom had, and the fourth oldest of the children my dad had. We did not have much let alone trying to keep lights and gas on, each month was a struggle for my mom. Food sometimes was scarce, but God always made away whether it was through family members such as my grandmother, friends, and even the local food pantries at times, more times than I would like to remember.

"Oh please, do not feel sorry for me because this is not what this book is about. God had and still do have a plan for my life."

While Attending Elementary School I was not popular nor did I have a lot of friends maybe 1 or 2. When I attended 7th and 8th grade I enjoyed Modern Dance, it was instructed by a beautiful teacher by the name of Mrs. Berry whom I liked and was encouraged by her to take the class both years. This got me out of my comfort zone.

Although History was not my favorite subject but was needed for me to graduate from 8th grade, My teacher Mr. Ashley made sure that I learned it. I learned all 50 states and their Capitols and of course all the Presidents of the United States in office order. I also had to memorize the Preamble to the Constitution.

In the spring of 1977, I graduated from eighth grade and during that Summer I accepted Jesus Christ as my personal Savior at a small Baptist church on the west side of Chicago. I sang in the choir and had the courage to lead a song with another choir member. In the fall of 1977, I attended High School.

In 1979 I joined another Baptist church with some of my family members. I sang in the choir there also; I always had a desire to be a part of a church and wanted to know more about Jesus Christ.

By this time, I did have a few friends but, Jesus Christ became my best friend. I would read my bible on the bus ride to school and back and right before I went bed. I realized that I could tell God all my thoughts, even though He knew them all and who I was.

I could talk to him freely as if He were standing right next to me and of course, He was. He was always there even when I felt alone, I was never alone.

I was just finishing up my sophomore year in high school and was dating my husband to be. It should have been a happy year for me, I even got a part-time job, but that year my sister under me died.

I went on to finish high school while working part-time at a small boutique about 6 blocks from my house. I enjoyed the walk there and back sometimes I would get a ride but during most days I walked.

During the last two years of high school, I made the honor roll three or four times and ranked in the top 100's out of approximately 600 students when I graduated. I think more children went to high school back then.

During high school, I was prescribed by my doctor to take birth control pills every day to correct a female problem that I was having. I was never good with swallowing pills although it was the smallest pill I had ever swallowed. I had a challenge remembering to take it daily sometimes, I would forget. I thinks it was because I had to do it daily and the thought of the taste when it started to dissolve in my mouth. I had other things that I would rather be doing than gagging on a pill every day.

I applied for college and was accepted but decided not to go away or go to college that year. I figured I needed to work and attend locally when I did decide to attend. I worked full time and paid rent of $100 to her grandmother whom my family moved in with so that we could help each other with the bills. I always was intrigued about traveling but never could really do it.

I enjoyed watching the airplanes take off and flying in the sky.

I decided that I would go to a two-year Business College and take up Travel Management this way I could still work and have bus fare to get back and forth and still help pay bills while living at home. I did not have a liken for typing nor did I like geography, but I still had a desire to learn it. Learning how to read a map was not one of my strong features but I knew if I was going to be in the travel world I needed to have some knowledge for direction for the sake of my career goal.

During my two years, I had to take geography twice to pass it. I always enjoyed Creative Writing even in grade school. This subject seemed to come easy for me because I could express my thoughts and dreams in writing even though I had a challenge with punctuation and still do today.

In August of 1985 in my Marketing class, we were given an assignment to, create a product, the marketing layout for it, including how we would transport our product to get it from one town to the next. my class was given maybe two weeks to complete the assignment.

I thought about it and ask God what I could create and get a good grade for creating it. After thinking about it one morning while forcing myself to take a birth control pill I got the answer. I said out loud, "I will write about a birth control pill that you would only take once every season" although at the time I was taking it to correct a female problem that I had every month. God even gave me the name for it, "The Seasonal Birth Control." Thank you, Lord!

I started writing and here is what I wrote without the misplaced or missing punctuations and misspelled words. I typed it so that you could get a clear picture of my writing. A copy of my original paper is in the back of this book.

(This is what I wrote)

THE FEMALE SEASONAL BIRTH CONTROL PILL

I am introducing the female Seasonal Birth Control pill. The ideal came from the original female birth control pill. There are several birth control methods available, such as the IUD, Condom, and Jell, which are just a few to name. But not one is more effective than the female Seasonal Birth Control pill.

"Remember I had to present, or should I say come up with a product, present it and then write how I would introduce or advertise it to the world in my report."

Since there was not much competition, the only major competition I could probably have is with the original birth control pill itself.

I figured females got tired of remembering every morning or every night to take their pill. Sometimes they even forgot it existed. And then there is an unwanted child to be born in this world if he or she is going to be born at all.

Some females get a sick feeling after taking the pill for a certain amount of time, where they felt that they could not any longer stomach it. The Seasonal pill is only meant to be taken every three months that is why it is called seasonal. This pill will stay in the female system for exactly three months. It will not stop her monthly menstrual cycle. Toward the end of the third month in the last week after her menstrual cycle, the female will experience a hot feeling when urinating. I advised the user not to panic when going through this.

"There were so many misspelled words in my original report that I would have given the report back and told me to correct the spelling. But I guess that it was not important to the instructor then the product that had been created."

I continued to write; My pill is just as effective as the original pill (98%). There is less risk of getting pregnant. Because of the hot feeling, you get in the third month and after your menstrual cycle while still taking the pill. The pill will let you know when you are pregnant and when it is time to stop taking the pill. If you are pregnant in between the three months and the pill is still in your system just like the original monthly pill it will not hurt, you or the baby.

Besides feeling faint or dizzy the symptom this pill gives you is a mint green discharge because the pill is green and has a minty taste and easy to swallow. This kind of discharge will only happen once to let you know what's happening, so you won't have to go out and buy the e.p.t(early pregnancy test) or pay extra money to see a doctor but you can, to make sure you and the baby are alright.

This pill can be used by ages eleven through forty, especially the teenagers. Because so many teenagers produce the most babies, I consider this pill would be great for younger teenagers. I think my pill would be especially important for this age group.

The Seasonal every *three-month birth control pill is very small just like the monthly pill is*. It comes in one shade(mint green). *It is just as effective as the monthly one which comes in several shades. Even though some months have only 28 days, this pill has the ingredients for 30 days each month, so do not worry.*

As I mentioned before it is a mint green color and has a minty taste, therefore, making it easy to swallow. It has no after taste unlike the original monthly pill.

You do not have to buy this pill monthly but yearly; the case contains four pills. It cannot be bought every three months but yearly. Soon as your fourth month is over with. You can have the next seasonal pill ready to take immediately.

"I stated that I had never been so embarrassed of my writing in this report and that even the wrong words were used such as brought which should have been bought." "I corrected it so that you can get the picture of what I was saying."

You can buy these pills in a long square case that reads, "THE SEASONAL BIRTH CONTROL PILL" on top label. The case is mint green and clicks open when pressing an arrow upwards, the arrow pointed notch opens better when pressed by your thumb.

Inside the case, each pill is divided and is covered with an extra special cotton layer so that no particles of dust can fall on them when you are opening it. The pill itself is mint green color as it has been stated through this report and is square-shaped. As you lift a pill out of its section it has a number 3,6,9 or 12 carved underneath it at the bottom of the case.

A small arrow points you where to start so that you may choose the lowest month first such as number 3. This lets you know which month you will be taking the next pill and when to order more. A pamphlet is Included on top of each cotton inside the case with instructions on how to take the pill with liquids, it may not be taken with alcohol.

The pamphlet gives instructions on how to take the pill and what will happen while taking them if you are pregnant and what kind of symptoms to expect.

When you buy The Seasonal pills, you will also receive an extra pamphlet just in case you misplace the one that comes inside the case. The extra pamphlet is also given to you for sharing to pass along to your friends or associates.

I also stated that I had never seen a paper so terribly written, misspelled words how could anyone allow this and not be corrected. He circled one misspelled word out of many.

My product is for all classes of people. The original birth control pill costs an average of fifteen dollars per month giving a total of one hundred eighty dollars per year. Since the seasonal birth control pill is bought once a year, The lower class will buy it for one hundred and sixty-five a case.

The middle class will purchase it for one hundred and seventy dollars per year. The upper class can purchase it for one hundred and eighty dollars.

When I looked at this report again after so many years ago, it was very discriminating and that I would only charge one price for all.

This product may only be purchased through a pharmacy and prescribed only by a qualified doctor one who can thoroughly explain the directions although they do come with the packet. My pill is safe to take because it has been checked by the Food and Drug Administrative (FDA) twice.

The Seasonal Birth Control Pill will be distributed to all the pharmacies in the United States. It would be transported by trucks that would be owned by me. It would be a mint green truck trimmed in white with the initials printed in large just like it would be in small print engraved on the pill. The pill will cost me one hundred and sixty dollars so I would sell it to the retailers three dollars a pack. I am not sure how many I would produce maybe as many that are called for.

This price does not make any since to me how I came up with these numbers I do not even know. I assume my teacher didn't know nor did he care.

To Introduce my product to the public I would use billboards and posters. I would have them posted in the drug stores, doctor offices, and hospitals. I would also use magazines, radio, and social media. In the magazines, there would be coupons for discounts for the product. Above each advertisement would be written including on my trucks "SEASONAL PILLS FOR NO SEASONAL BABIES".

I was told by my class instructor that I had received the highest grade in my class for my paper, it a **B+**. This brings tears to my eyes, happy I passed but not how with so many errors in misspelled words. It seems to me he did not care about the girl from the westside of Chicago only about her great idea. Again, I say he did not care enough to return my paper back to me so that I could correct the errors. I forgive him.

I do not think it was a racist move just a selfish take advantage one. It was an uneducated or ignorant one on my part had I known to protect my idea I would have.

This concludes my story I went on with my life still writing many books of course with an editor and using spelling and punctuation apps. I also learned that I was diagnosed with Ovarian Cancer in my middle 30's and was healed through the Word of God! Without surgery and without Chemotherapy. I am Victorious! what A Mighty God I serve.

I later saw that there was a birth control pill that was produced called, "Seasonale" and then changed later to "Seasonique", Well now, could it be???

I tried to get lawyers to investigate the matter but because the time was over 30 years ago no one would be bold enough to touch it and I had no knowledge about patent back then. Who protects the innocent and uneducated? But God.

THE FEMALE SEASONAL BIRTHCONTROL PILL

I am introducing the female seasonal birthcontrol pill. The ideal
came from the orininal female birthcontrol pill. Ever since man became
aware of the relationship between sexual intercourse and conception, he
has searched for some method mechanical, medicinal, magical-- which
would prevent pregnancy or limitation of offspring for whatever reasons,
ill health, econocics planned spacing of child birth, or personal reasons--
should be the mutual decision of the partners concerned. There are
several birthcontrol methods available, such as the iud, condum, and
jell, are just a few to name. But not one is more effective than the
female seasonal birthcontrol pill. Because there isn't there's not
much competition. The only major competition I could probably have is
with the original birthcontrol pill itself.

I figure females get tired of remembering every morning or every
night to take their pill. Sometimes they even forget it exsist. And
then there's an unwanted child to be born in this world if its going
to be born. Some females get a sick feeling after taking the pill for
a certain amount of time, where they feel that they can't no longer
stomach it. The seasonal pill only has to be taken every three months
(thats why it is called seasonal). This pill will stay in the female
system exactly three months. Toward the end of the third month in the
last week (after the menstrual cycle). The female will experience a
hot feeling when urinating. I advise the user not to panick when going
through this.

THE FEMALE SEASONAL BIRTHCONTROL PILL

My pill is just as effective as the original pill (98%). There is less risk in getting pregnant. Because of the hot feeling you get (in the third month and after your menstrual cycle) while still taking the pill. The pill also let you know when you are pregnant and that it's time to stop taking the pill. If so you are pregnant in between the three months and the pill is still in your system, just like the monthly pill it won't hurt you or the baby. Besides feeling faint or dizzy the symton, this pill gives you is a mint green discharge(because the pill is of that color with a minty taste easy to digest). This kind of discharge will only happen once to let you know whats happening, so you won't have to go out and buy the e.p.t (early pregnancy test) or pay extra money to see a doctor but can, to make sure the baby and you are alright.

This pill can be used by ages eleven through forty, especially the teenagers. Because so many teenagers produce the most babies, which I consider is an early age I think my pill would be very important for this particular age group. The three month birth control pill is small in size just as the monthly one. It comes in one color(mint green), which is just as effective as the monthly one which come in several shades. Even though some months have only 28 days, this pill has the ingrediants for 30 days each month, so don't worry. As I mentioned befor it is mint because it has a minty taste to it as you begin to swallow it (makes it easy to digest). It has no after taste where is the monthly pill do. You can only buy this pill yearly (the case contains four pills).

THE FEMALE SEASONAL BIRTHCONTROL PILL

It can not be brought every three months only so you won't have
to worry about going out every three months to purchase them and so
that as soon as your third month is over with , you have them right at
your hand, and can pop one into your mouth immediately. You buy these
pills in a long square case that says "THE SEASONAL BIRTHCONTROL PILL"
on top label. The case is mint green and clicks open when pressing an
arrow upwards,the arrow pointed notch opens better when pressed by thumb.

Inside the case each pill is divided and is covered with a extra
special cotton so that no particlesof dust or dirt can not fall on them
when you are opening. The pill has my initals on them(M.R.P)carved on
them in dark green,but the pill itself is mint green ,as has been stated
through this report. As one lift a pill out of its section it has a
number 3,6,9,or 12 also carved in the back ground of the case.
An arrow shows where to start at so that you may lift up the lowest
month first. And that will let you know what month you're going to take
and have left so that when you are on month 12 you know automatically
its time to buy some more ,same as the monthly one, when you run out
or take the last one. Also located on top of the cotton inside the
case there as a little pathlet with instructions,on how to take the pill
with any kind of liquid other than liquor. When they are suppose to be
taken is also written in this pathlet it also tells you what will
happen while taking them and if you are pregnant what kind of symtons
to expect. When buying the seasonal pills you will also receive
an extra pathlet just in case you misplace the one that comes with
the case.. The extra one also is given to you for advertising
so that you might share and past on to your friends or associates
so that they may know about the seasonal pill. I am sure they'll want
to know about it.

THE FEMALE SEASONAL BIRTHCONTROL PILL

I should also mention even though it isn't that much important, the pill is a small square shape one. My product is aiming at the lower-class, middle-class, upper-class people. Since the original birthcontrol pill costs about fifthteen per month which adds up to one-hundred and eighty dollars a year. Since my product is not brought every month but once a year. I will sell it to the lower-class for one-hundred and sixty-five a case. And since its very hard for some of them to pruchase them still. Those who have medical cards can receive them with their card.

I will sell it to the middle-class for ten dollars more which is one-hundred and seventy dollars, because I figure the middle-class makes nine-thousand and up to about sixteen thousand. The upper-class will be paying also ten dollars more I figured they could pay about that much which is one-hundred and eighty dollars, which also is about the price of the monthly pill would add up in a year. Because I am aiming at the three groups this is called the multi-segment. I will be earning five dollars off each case I sell to the lower-class people(it cost me one-hundred and sixty dollars to produce the pills and case plus the advertising). I will earn ten dollars more from the middle-class people. I will earn fifthteen dollars more and it will cost them ten dollars more than the lower-class peoples. It will cost the upper-class peoples five dollars more than the middle-class, making it twenty dollars more than the lower-class people.

This product may only be purchased by a phymacy and prescribed only by a qualified doctor, so that he or she may explain to their patient how the pill works exactly. Even though the instruction come with them upon purchasing. This product can be sold by any qualified phymacy and doctor.

THE FEMALE SEASONAL BIRTHCONTROL PILL

My pill is safe to take because it has been checked by the Food and Drug Administratives. The product will be distribute to any phymacy in the United States. It will be transported by trucks because its cheaper and the trucks will be own by me the producer. It will be painted in mint green and trimmed in white,with the initials M.B.P printed in large just like it will be in small print engraved on the pill. The pill will cost me one-hundred and sixty dollars so I'll sell it to the retailers three dollars a pack (Not sure how many I'm going to produce).

In introducing my product to the public I will use billboards that will be posted in drugstores and doctor's offices as well as hospitals too. I will also use the teen magazines to reach the teenagers. In these teen magazines there will be free cut out coupons that will say "SEASONAL PILLS for NO SEASONAL BABIES" this theme will also be printed on my bilboards. And at the bottom of this coupon it will say take it to your nearest doctor for your free sample.

www.ingramcontent.com/pod-product-compliance
Lightning Source LLC
Chambersburg PA
CBHW060841270326
41933CB00002B/158